Football For Beginners:

Essential Training and Game Tactics Tips For Playing and Coaching

By

Charles Maldonado

Table of Contents

Introduction 5

Chapter 1. American Football in a Nutshell 7

Chapter 2. History and Evolution of Football....................... 9

Chapter 3. Popularity of American Football and Worth of The NFL 12

Chapter 4. Main Rules and Dimensions of The Game 14

    The Football Field and the Football 14

    The Teams within The Teams 17

    Getting The Game Started and Continuing it 22

Chapter 5. Playing Tips and Playing Strategies 25

    Offensive Strategy and Formation 25

    Defensive Strategy and Formation 28

    Special Teams Strategy 30

Chapter 6. Training Tips 32

Conclusion 38

Thank You Page 40

Football For Beginners:

Essential Training and Game Tactics Tips For Playing and Coaching

By Charles Maldonado

© Copyright 2014 Charles Maldonado

Reproduction or translation of any part of this work beyond that permitted by section 107 or 108 of the 1976 United States Copyright Act without permission of the copyright owner is unlawful. Requests for permission or further information should be addressed to the author.

This publication is designed to provide accurate and authoritative information in regard to the subject matter covered. This work is sold with the understanding that the publisher is not engaged in rendering legal, accounting, or other professional services. If legal advice or other expert assistance is required, the services of a competent professional person should be sought.

First Published, 2014

Printed in the United States of America

Introduction

Playing sports is a worldwide phenomenon. You can look at any part of the world, rich or poor, and you will see that they too have a certain sport they all are fond of. And in some countries they have more than 1 sport with a large fan following. There may be 1 national sport but many will also closely follow other sports taking place in the country. For most people these sports have a large impact on their lives. Not only do they take out time from their busy schedules to get together to play these games in a friendly manner like on family outings. But workdays are spent dreaming about their favorite team and when they will be playing next. Large amount of money is spent on going to games and on buying official merchandise. For these people this sport becomes their life.

Though many people may not have that much time to play their favorite sports themselves due to other commitments in their lives. They will surely take out time to watch it. In the United States, there are many sports with a large fan following including baseball, basketball and so on. But hands down the most watched and the most popular sport in the United

States is football. Not only is it popular at the professional and national level, but also at the college and high school level.

Chapter 1. American Football in a Nutshell

American football (known as just football in the U.S) is a rugby styled game which is played between two teams, with 11 players each, with an oval shaped ball known as the football. It is played on a rectangular field with all goal posts at each end and floor markings in white on the ground. The team, which has control over the ball, is known as the offense team for the period they have the ball and the team without the control of the ball is known as the defense team, for the period they do not have the ball. The purpose of the offense team is to try to cover as much ground on the field with the ball by either passing the ball to teammates or a certain player running across the field with the ball. The defense team, as the name suggests, will try to act as a barrier and will try to stop the offense team from making much ground and stop them from reaching the goalpost or the end zone. In this entire process, the defense teams main aim will be to try to get possession of the football so that they can then try to score points with the ball.

To start with, the offense team is given 4 'downs' (chances) to try to advance at least 10 yards. If they are successful, then they are given 4 more downs, but if they are unsuccessful then they have to hand over the ball to the opposing team and then the opposing team is given 4 plays to advance at least 10 yards and so on. The whole purpose of this is to score points as at the end of the game the team with the most points wins. Points can be scored in the following ways:

- Any player advances into the opposing teams end zone with the football. This is known as a touchdown.

- Any player kicks the football over and across the opponent's goal post. This is known as a field goal.

- The ball carrier of the offense team is tackled in his own end zone. This is known as a safety.

Chapter 2. History and Evolution of Football

American football takes it roots from rugby and earlier forms of it started to be played in the 1860's. Like ice hockey and basketball, this sport too was first developed on college campuses as different colleges would meet up each year and play each other in a game that was similar to rugby. The first recorded American football game was played on November 6th 1869, between Rutgers and Princeton and was played with rules coming from both rugby and soccer. Playing like this continued for some while, but then soon after the sporting representatives got tired of this game play and representatives of Harvard, Columbia, Princeton and Yale met up and molded the rules of the games so that they would suit their own needs and specifications. This was later on known as the Massoit Convention of 1876 and it also laid the foundation for the Inter Collegial Football Association.

Over the years more and more people started to gain interest in this sport and it started to be played more and more. Head coach at Yale, Walter Camp, who is thought of as the 'Father of Football' introduced many changes to the game which include:

- The numbers of players were reduced from 15 to 11.

- Points allotted to a touchdown were 6 points.

- Introduction of 'downs', better understood as plays or chances a team has to advance forward with the ball or the ball has to be passed over to the opposing team. This is an important difference between rugby and American football.

- Replacing the chaotic and dangerous scrum with the snap (which is a backwards pass)

These introductions made by Camp, greatly influenced the game and have played an important part in shaping it into the game that we see now days. But needless to say Yale has had much influence on American football, as the first ever football players recorded too was from Yale. William Heffelfinger was the first player to be paid a certain amount in November 1892 to play in a game for the AAA (Allegheny Athletic Association) versus their rivals the Pittsburgh Athletic Club.

In 1910, some sort of a Professional League emerged but it was disorganized and the players did not know loyalty, as they would move from team to team offering their footballing services. So in 1920 an American Professional Football Association was developed, which was later renamed National Football League (NFL) in 1922. The whole purpose of this was to look over the game and to see that certain rules were made and players and teams both followed them. In the 1960's The American Football League emerged headed by Lamar Hunt, due to which there were constant fights and bickers between the two leagues. Then before the starting of the 1970 league, both these were merged and formed one National Football League but with 2 leagues: American Football Conference and the National Football Conference. The winner of each of these leagues would face each other in one final face off championship match known as the Super Bowl and the winner of this match would be named the National Champion.

Chapter 3. Popularity of American Football and Worth of The NFL

Without a doubt, American football is the most popular sport of the United States and has fans glued to their Television sets every Friday and Saturday afternoon as well as on Sunday and Monday nights. Though it is an American sport and most known about in the US, still it happens to be the most lucrative sport worldwide with an annual revenue of 9.5 billion dollars, out of which 5 billion dollars comes from television alone. The reason for such high revenues can be accounted from mass TV exposure and deals with famous television channels such as FOX, ESPN and so on. The National championship game, the Super Bowl, is the most watched sports event around the globe and the Super Bowl in 2010 was the most watched T.V program in the history of the U.S. Also this is because since September 2010, football matches accounted for 55% of the T.V programs that had more than 20 million viewers. Another reason for this is that each football game has many people attending it with an average attendance of 67,604 so a part of the revenue does stem from ticket sales as well. In addition to all this, another major factor for the high revenue is the sales coming from the sales of the official merchandise. Ever die-hard fan wants something from the Official merchandise store, be it a replica shirt or a flag or any other thing. Buying merchandise has become a necessity for every fan and with different companies coming out with new and innovative products each day it is no wonder that sales from merchandise are sky rocketing as well.

When we look at the worth of the NFL beyond the revenue it brings in, we see that the NFL teams make up 60% of 'The World's 50 Most Valuable Sports Team. Thirty out of the fifty teams in this list are from the NFL, which just goes to show how lucrative and expensive this league is. And this is a fact which cannot be ignored when you look at the bigger picture, which is that American football is not even that popular worldwide and still it is able to bring in such high revenues is clearly something amazing.

Chapter 4. Main Rules and Dimensions of The Game

Football stems off from rugby and this can clearly be seen by how similar the two games look especially if you do not know much about both. Football is as much about gaining territory and trying to cross over into the opposing teams part of the field as it is about scoring points. It is a battle for each yard of field there is in the hope to get a touchdown or score a field goal. The main purpose of the game is to defend the part of the field behind you and stop the opposing team to reach into your end zone with the ball and scoring and at the same time trying to take the ball away from the opposing team and treading over their part of the field trying to reach their end zone to score points for your team. Now we will look at some major aspects of the game to get a better understanding of it.

The Football Field and the Football

In this section let's look at the general features of an American Football field and the football used to play it as without these two things the game could not be played properly. When looking at the field we see that it is a 100-yard field with different types of white markings on it. The white small markings indicate an inch of the field and after every 5 inches there is a solid white line running across the entire field width wise. After every 10 inches there is also a solid white line just like the 5 inch marking, the only difference is that for every 10 inches there is also a number written next to it to specify how many yards have been covered. On each side of the field, which runs the whole length of the area, there is a 6-foot wide area known as the sideline. Running the entire width of the area and connecting the two sidelines there is also a 6-foot wide area that is known as the end line. At both ends of the field, length wise, there is a 10 yards area known as the end zone, here all the points are scored. In the center of the end zone there is a 10 feet pole with a horizontal cross bar with ribbons attached that is the goal post and the goal line is the 8-inch wide line running lengthwise at the front of the end zone.

Moving on to the football, the football has a unique oblong sphere shape and is a type of ball that is different from all other balls. The Official National Football League (NFL) ball is hand made by the company 'Wilson Sporting Goods Co.' and length-wise it is around 11-11.5 inches long and the circumference is 28.5. The circumference width-wise is 21.5 inches wise and an average football weighs between 397 grams to 425 grams. The inside of the ball is made up of an inflated polyurethane bladder that is covered with cowhide as protection. So the outside of the ball is of leather which is sewn together using synthetic lining and then it is laced with cotton covered in vinyl. The bladder inside has a valve, which protrudes outside through the leather, and it is this valve that is used to pump air into the bladder causing it to inflate and making it ready to use.

The Teams within The Teams

Each NFL team is allowed to have a maximum of 53 players on the team and only 11 of these players can be on the field at one given time during a match. Teams are allowed to make substitutions throughout the game so that they can fully utilize the strengths of each player at the time needed, though the substitutions can only be made during the teams own 'downs'. Every team consists of three teams, which can be considered as units. So every team has an offense unit, defense unit and a special team. Together these units work together to create an efficient manner of game play as well as of trying to score points.

Offense Team

As we have discussed earlier, the main role of the offense team is to try to advance on to the opponent's part of the field as much as they can in order to be able to cross into the opponent's end zone so that points can be scored. This can either be done by passing the ball from player to player or one player could just hold the ball and keep on running forward (and avoiding collisions with the defense team on the way) trying to gain as much territory of the opponent's field with the ball in hand. There are many different offensive positions in which a player can play. The quarterback (or the field general/leader) is responsible for passing the ball either to the receiver or to the running backs. Receivers are players whose responsibility is to run down the field and catch the balls the quarter back throws towards them. Depending on their positioning they are called wide receivers or tight receivers. On the other hand, the responsibility of the running backs is to take the ball from the quarterback and run up the field with it. According to the formation of the team the running backs can be either a tailback, half back or full back. Lastly, we have the offensive linemen who are there so that they can provide protection to the quarter back and running backs. They do this by blocking off any incoming players from the defense team. There are three types of offensive linemen: Center, guards, and tackles. Centers are in the middle of the field, while the 2 guards flank the center offensive linemen. The 2 tackles are to the outside of the 2 guards. Together these 5 players form the protection unit of the offense team.

Defense Team

The defense team, as talked about earlier, is the team that does not have the possession of the ball. Their main purpose is to block off all advances from the offense team and try to block off their plays so that the offense team cannot move forward in to the defense's part of the field. Also the defense team will try their best that the opponents are not allowed to enter their end zone and take away some points. While doing all this, the defense team will also be trying to gain possession of the ball. There are 4 types of players in the defense team. The defense linemen try to tackle down the quarterback before he is able to either pass the ball or hand over the ball to his teammates. Also the defense linemen are supposed to stop the running backs from carrying the play forward. There are 3 to 4 linemen: the left/right end linemen line up outside and try to confuse the offensive tackles. The nose tackle is responsible to line around the football and keep their focus on the ball. The left/right defense tackle position themselves opposite to the guards and break the offensive line. The second types of players, known as the linebackers, are there to provide back up for the linemen. They consist of runners and cover the offense receivers on some plays. If there are 4 linemen then there is 1 middle line backer and 2 outside linebackers. But if there are 3 linemen, then there are 2 inside 2 linebackers and 2 outside linebackers. Then there are the cornerbacks, who try to break up the passes coming from the quarterback so as to prevent the receivers from getting the ball. Lastly there are safeties, which play deep onto the field and try to stop the offense team from making long passes or runs. There is a strong safety, which plays to the side where there are more offensive players and then there is a free safety, which plays in the deep, middle position.

Special Teams

The Special team unit of the team comes into play when a team has to kick the ball and it includes the kickers of the team, the offensive line and the players responsible for tackling a returner. These include the placekicker who tries to kick the ball through the goalposts in the end zone to score points for his team. He also kicks the ball to the other team to start the game and after each scoring point. Then there is the punter who free kicks the ball if his team is unable to advance the ball down the field. Lastly, the returner is the one who at the time of the kickoff tries to catch the ball so that he can return it as far as he can. It is possible that a player is able to score a touchdown on a return play.

Getting The Game Started and Continuing it

Having looked at all the players involved in the game, now let's look at how the game starts and is then continued. First and foremost a coin takes place to decide that which time will first receive the opening kickoff of the game. Once this happens both teams fight for the possession of the ball, so as to become the offense team on the field. Ball possession can be achieved in the following ways:

- By receiving a kick off – At the start of each half and after conceding a goal from the other team, your team receives a kickoff.

- Turnover – This is when the defense team is able to get the ball from the offense team by chance by either a fumble or interception. A fumble is when the offense team drops the ball and the defense team is able to pick it up while an interception is when a ball thrown by the offense quarterback is picked by the defense.

-Safety – The player with the all possession is tackled the end zone they were defending, so the ball automatically goes to the other team through a free kick.

-Turnover on downs – This is the failure of the offense team to advance the ball ten yards in the 4 downs and as a result they have to forfeit the ball to their opponent.

-Punt – This is when the defense is able to stop the offense from advancing 10 yards in 3 downs. So then the offense free kicks or punts the ball to their opponent on the third down.

Moving on, remember about the downs or plays discussed earlier? After each down, the officials look at the field and measure how many yards a team has gained or lost. Yards are lost when the player holding the ball is tackled behind the line of scrimmage, which is an imaginary line running across the width of the field and is the point up till where the offense team advances with the ball. This then becomes the starting point from where the next down for the offence team starts. If a team fails to reach the 10-yard mark after the 3 downs then they can either punt the ball to their opponents or try their one last chance to get to the 10-yard mark in the 4th down. If they are able to then they will get more downs but if not they have to forfeit the ball to the opposing team. Sometimes the offense time prefers to punt the ball as this way their opponents will have to cover a larger distance on the field to try to score points. At this time the opponent can take the ball and make a return with it, which means that they can catch it and run across the field with it. But the other team will be hoping to tackle them and stop them from scoring points.

Scoring Points

There are different ways that points can be scored. First we have the touchdown in which you can get 6 points if you are able to reach the end line of the opponents end zone. You can get an extra 1-point if you are able to kick the ball through the goal posts after a touchdown. A 2-point conversion occurs if you are able to advance into the opponent's end zone with the ball. A field goal is when you are able to kick the ball through the opponent's goalposts and this can give you 3 points. The last way to score points is by a safety and this is when you can bring down your opponent with the ball in the opponents own end zone. In all the above cases, except safety, after scoring points the ball has to be free kicked to the opponent. When you score a safety you will get the ball with a free kick.

Chapter 5. Playing Tips and Playing Strategies

Each team has their own set of players and a coach and other people helping out the coach. All these people combined together, think of the best strategies to use so that they are able to maximize the certain skills a player has. There are different strategies that can be used and some will be discussed here.

Offensive Strategy and Formation

In the offensive strategy, most players are chosen on how well they can do run blocking as well as how good they are at rush skills. Another name for a run oriented offense is called a ball control offense. Running teams are good at time wasting in the sense that most of their plays lead to a lot of time being used and in this way not only does their defense get to rest for longer but it makes it easier for them to hold onto a lead. The only downside to this strategy is that, if they fall behind points wise, then it is hard for them to get back into the game. Another strategy in the offense unit is when most of the players are skilled at pass blocking. Teams that use this pass blocking strategy usually can score a lot and are great at coming up from behind, but since they do not know how to use up all the clock time available there is always a fear of them losing by a turnover made by their opponents. A mix of both the run blocking and pass blocking would be an ideal strategy to be followed.

Over the years many formations have come to exist and each is used in different situations. Some managers prefer a certain formation over the other while others might not find the same formation that appealing. The shotgun formation is a popular offensive formation in which the quarterback stands a lot further behind the line of scrimmage than he usually does. This formation is quite advantageous as the quarterback gets a lot more protection from the offensive linemen, as they are able to better protect the quarterback from the defense blitzing him. If the quarterback has enough speed and mobility, then he use this formation to scramble a bit before he is to pass the ball. But in this formation, the defense is almost sure that a pass will come resulting in a haphazard snap rather than the normal pass of the ball. There is also a wishbone offensive strategy in which there is a triple option with a lead blocker and the quarterback takes the snap from the center and has a full back and 2 half backs or tail backs protecting him, giving the quarterback more space for movement. The full back is behind the quarterback and the halfbacks are behind the fullback, one is a little to the right, while the other is to the left and that makes a wishbone formation. Another formation is known as the wildcat formation and in this formation any other player from another position apart from the quarterback rushes in to receive the snap. So in a way this formation confuses the defense, as it is difficult to identify when the offense will use the wildcat. If the defense is able to identify that a wildcat is about to be used than defending becomes quite easy. Now we will look at the pistol offense in which the quarterback is positioned to be 4 yards (rather than the usual 7 yards) behind the center and then the running back positions himself only 3 yards behind the quarterback. In this strategy the quarterback is close enough to the defense to figure out what formation the defense might be using but he is also far enough to get a better view of the field and see where he is to pass the ball.

Defensive Strategy and Formation

In the defensive strategy, a blitz is commonly used. The blitz is used against a pass and it is when a player tries to rush the passer of the opposing team so that they have less time to pass and there is always a chance that the pass is miscalculated. Multiple players can do blitz but that just means that there would now be less players playing on the downfield covering tackles and runners and that too is a disadvantage. Another strategy is known as the prevent defense and can be done later on in the game and the whole purpose of this strategy is to pressurize the opponents into making short runs and passes, so that they are unable to make long passes.

Basic defense formations are described by numbers and are in the order number of linemen and then the number of linebackers. The number of defensive backs used is usually not mentioned in the formation but if they were then the defense formation would look something like this:

(no. of linemen – no. of linebackers- no. of defense backs).

So a number like 4-2-5 would mean that for the play the defense is using 4 linemen, 2 linebackers and 5 defense backs.

The most common defense formations are the 4-3 or the 3-4. Though they are somewhat similar, in the 3-4 a linemen is removed and a defense back is added. This is done so that the 3 linemen can keep the opponents offensive line busy, while the 4 linebackers depending on the situation on hand either rush the quarter back into making a 'wrong' pass or they go further back for more deeper coverage. Another formation is the 3-3-5 and is also known as the spread defense. In this the defense confuses the offense by random multiple blitzing. Though it may seem as this is a good formation, it is not that popular at the NFL level, but highly popular at the college or high school level. Dime defense is also a defensive strategy in which 6 defensive backs are used (usually 2 safeties and 4 corner backs). This is a strategy used against teams who prefer passing the ball and as a result the defense uses this to prevent the offense from making medium to long range passes.

Special Teams Strategy

Special teams is that part of the team which only comes into action when they are required to make kickoffs, take free kicks, do punts or make a field goal. As the risk of injury is high in these situations, the starting offensive and defensive players usually do not play in the special team positions. For the kickoff an onside strategy can be used in which the ball is kicked in such a way that it covers a very short distance and the team can regain instant possession. This is usually done in situations when the team is losing and needs to score points. Another strategy is the squib or pooch kick. This strategy is there to confuse your opponents as in this the ball is kicked in such a way that it hits the ground and then bounces, making it difficult to determine which way the ball is going. It is best used when you want to avoid conceding points on returns.

Moving on to punts, we can use the fake punt strategy in which you are trying to deceive the offense in such a way that you are able to either score points or can advance a lot on the field. This fake punt strategy is similar to the fake field goal strategy. In the fake field goal, the players assume their positions like normal but they don't hold the ball for a kick, but instead the layers either runs with the ball, makes a short pass to a nearby player or attempts to throw the ball down the field. Both these strategies are highly risky, but if performed correctly, then they prove to be beneficial.

Chapter 6. Training Tips

After going through all this, it is easy to figure out that American football is an aggressive sport and requires a lot of physical exertion. Also one has to admit that along with being a sport, playing football is actually one major workout itself. This is a sport that involves constant movement, mostly running and pushing and shoving for the entire game. So how do these players, whether they are playing at the professional level or not, keep themselves physically fit to play this physically strenuous sport?

The answer: Training!

For all major workouts, warm up exercises are a must so that the body is mentally as well as physically ready for the upcoming workout. In the same way workout exercises are an essential aspect for any player who wants to build up the physical strength required to play this game on a constant basis. So before any training a player should make sure that he has warmed up to avoid getting pulling a muscle during the training.

Physical fitness is a must for a football player as a physically fit player would not only give a great performance but they will also be less susceptible to injuries on the field. That is why it is important that there is mid season as well as off-season training. Mid season training can be done a day after the game in which there are quick paced workouts and low amounts of weights. Then some days later, when you have recovered from the fatigue of the game do a more extensive workout with heavier weights. Doing all this will make sure that you are physically fit throughout the season. Offseason training is important as well, as not only does it help you stay health and fit when you are not playing, but also it helps you improve on your body strengths so that you can play better on the field. You can do extreme workouts in the weight rooms as well as go out on the field and practice your runs. A combination of these two will help you prepare for the upcoming season.

Now we will look a bit closer at some training exercises. Football requires a large amount of body strength to be able to go on. Apart from being able to complete the time on the field, body strength is also required in order to outrun or tackle your opponent and take possession from them. To break it down, lower body strength is required for activities such as kicking, turning etc. While upper body strength is required for ball throwing, fighting off opponents etc.

Role of strength exercises

So where does all this body strength come from? It of course comes from exercise. Strength exercises are an essential part of any players training and they are also done as a preparation for matches. This is because these strength exercises help build up muscles as well as lean muscle mass which in turn provides the body with strength to cope with the physical side of this sport. These exercises are mostly used to build up muscles in the legs, as legs are the most active part of the body during football.

Squats

Squats are one of the most common strength exercises as doing these helps strengthen the leg muscles. You do these by standing up right with your spine straight and your feet at shoulders width apart. Make sure that your buttocks are sticking out and then gradually lower your upper body until it reaches your knees and then get back up again. This whole cycle will complete one squat and three sets of 10 squats should get your leg muscles up and going.

Sprints

Sprinting is generally regarded as a cardio exercise but many players prefer doing sprint exercises as it has muscle building capabilities especially in the quads and your hamstrings. Two days of concentrated sprinting sessions in one week should help increase your muscle mass.

Uphill runs

Uphill runs are an effective way to build up muscle and strengthen the body. It involves sprinting up the hill but slowly jogging while coming down the hill. This exercise does seem vigorous and it is, but it does yield quicker results. Repeat this 5-10 times, depending on your stamina and you will feel those muscles building up.

Power Jumps

As the name suggests, power jumps are quick jumps with a lot of force so that you can go a little higher than when you are usually jumping. They are a really good way of building leg muscles especially in the quadriceps, hamstrings and calves. 5 sets of 20 power jumps should do the trick and after continuous exercise you will be able to feel that you can run faster and kick even harder.

Speed Training

Apart from body strength, speed is an important part of the game as well. That is why it is essential that a player does speed training as well so that they can keep up with the speed of the game. The best way to do this is to do sprint trainings. You can do these using cones (zig zag), going uphill or downhill or just with friends. But remember to do sprint training for just 25-30 minutes, as this is the best way to get the most out of these training exercises. Any time more will just put extra burden on your body and the whole purpose of this will be lost. Another important thing to remember is that you should do these speed training during the off season training as it is the best time to build up your speed and agility and get you prepared for the upcoming season.

Reminders

There are many other strength building exercises such as chin-ups, crunches, bench pressing and so on. But always remember to warm up and warm down properly before and after your workout sessions respectively. Also remember to vary your exercise routines so there is no monotony. Lastly, the most important thing to know regarding football fitness is that fitness for playing football can best be achieved by playing football. So go out, kick that ball and show your skills.

Conclusion

American football may just a thing of America, but there is no doubt that it is one of the highest revenue bearing sport as a result of which its impact on the sporting world cannot be ignored. Though it takes its roots from rugby, over the years it has been molded to meet certain needs and as a result it is seen as a complete different sport from rugby.

But like rugby it too is a physically demanding sport and that is why each player should do all they can do upkeep their physical health to meet the demands of the games. So eating healthy and a healthy lifestyle should be adopted and exercise must be introduced into your routines so as to become strong enough for the game. Upper body strength is an area you should focus on as well as being able to coordinate with others where ball passing is concerned. Also learn how to be able to block off your opponent and be able to run with the ball with precision. All of these things will take practice and it is always good to practice with someone, preferably your team. But always remember to properly warm up before any game or workout so that you can get the best out of it.

Though to an outsider this sport might seem a bit confusing at the start, but a little patience while going over the rules and the point scoring will help you a lot in understanding how this game play works. But even if it doesn't, at times just watching the players play and the fans cheering their favorite teams on is a pleasure to watch in itself.

Thank You Page

I want to personally thank you for reading my book. I hope you found information in this book useful and I would be very grateful if you could leave your honest review about this book. I certainly want to thank you in advance for doing this.

www.ingramcontent.com/pod-product-compliance
Lightning Source LLC
LaVergne TN
LVHW021743060526
838200LV00052B/3435